First Book of
MAGIC

Written by Linda Stephenson
Illustrated by Heather Clarke

© 1993 Henderson Publishing Limited

Make a Magic Table

Before you begin to put your Magic Act together, you will need a magic table. To make a simple one, you'll need:

two strong cardboard boxes • scissors • glue • wrapping paper or a tablecloth

1 Remove the lid flaps from the boxes.

2 Glue the two boxes together, as shown.

3 Stick the cut out flaps on to the top of the table to reinforce it.

4 Cover the boxes with either the wrapping paper or a table cloth. Make sure you leave a gap at the back of the table, so you can store your props inside the boxes.

5 If you use paper, make yourself a jazzy sign with your name on it to stick on the front of your table so everyone will know who you are.

This table will also double as a place to keep your magic props when you are not using them.

Make a Magic Wand

Now for your magic wand.

You will need:
a coloured drinking straw • about nine pieces of uncooked spaghetti • sticky tape • scissors

1 Put the spaghetti inside the straw to make it firm.

2 Trim the ends of the spaghetti so they are the same size as the straw.

3 Block off the ends of the straw with the sticky tape, so the spaghetti doesn't fall out.

Magic wands are usually black with white tips. This is because they were originally made from ebony and ivory. But you can make your wand any colour you like.

To make a vanishing magic wand, just follow the above instructions, but leave out the spaghetti. Hold up the wand, cover with roll of newspaper and crumple in your hands. Your magic wand will vanish in the paper, as it will crumple with it.

First Book of Magic

 # Greedy Pig

Now for some tricks.

Hold up a paper bag and tip out four flat chewy sweets. Show that the bag is empty. Tell everyone that a greedy magician was supposed to share these sweets with a friend but decided to eat them all. (You take sweets out of their wrappers and eat them if you want!) When the friend came along the magician had to do some quick magic to find some sweets for her.

Put the wrappers back in the bag and hold the top tightly closed. Wave your wand and tear the bag open near the bottom. Four more sweets will fall out.

The Secret
You make a false bottom for the bag and conceal the four other sweets there. All you need do is to glue a smaller bag inside a larger bag, once you have put the sweets inside.

Five Alive

Ask someone to think of a number between 1 and 10.

Gaze into their eyes, then write the number 5 down on a piece of paper and put it in an envelope. Ask the person to hold the envelope.

Now ask them to double the number, add 10, divide it by 2 and then take away the number they first thought of. The answer will always be 5.

Ask the person to open the envelope. They will be amazed at your prediction.

The Secret
There is no secret, just a mathematical puzzle. Provided you give the person the right instructions, the answer will always be 5. But don't give it away as it will spoil the fun.

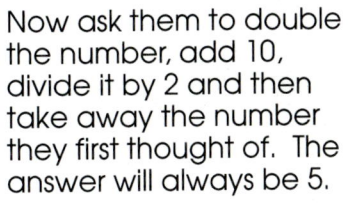

First Book of Magic

Crinkle Picture Illusion

You will need:
tracing paper • pencil • felt tipped pens • sheets of plain paper • scissors • a ruler • glue

1 Trace these two pictures, transfer them onto plain paper and colour them.

2 Now, using a ruler, divide the pictures into strips 1cm wide.

3 Cut the pictures into strips, making sure you don't get the pictures mixed up.

6 First Book of Magic

4 Fold a wide piece of paper, the same height as your pictures, into pleats 1cm wide.

5 Glue the strips from picture 1 onto the left facing pleats. Glue picture 2 strips onto the right hand ones.

6 If you look from the left, you will see the magician about to pull something from his hat.

7 If you look from the right, you will see it is a rabbit.

First Book of Magic

Track Jack

You show your audience a large sheet of thick paper. On it, you have drawn nine equal squares. In each square you have drawn various playing cards but in the very centre square is a Jack of Hearts. You ask someone from the audience to help you.

You tell the story of the Jack of Hearts who stole his mother's tarts and then hid amongst the other cards, so he wouldn't be caught. But you are a super detective and will catch him.

You fold the paper along all the lines, then ask your helper to tear out the squares as neatly as possible, then place them, face down, on a table. The helper then moves the pieces around so you cannot possibly know which piece is which. The paper must be thick enough so you can't see anything through it.

Now, waving your hands over the paper, you make a big show of tracking the thief by magic. You select a piece and, when it is turned over, it is Jack. How did you do it? Do you really have X-ray eyes?

No way! The secret is that the Jack piece of paper is the only piece that is torn on all four sides! So you should be able to pick it out easily!

 # Sad Sid

For this trick, you show your audience a drawing of a face. It is a Sad Sid's face. You say you will cheer him up with a joke. It can be a really good joke or your worst one. It's up to you.

You fold up the paper, crack the joke, then unfold the paper again. To everyone's amazement, Sad Sid is now Smiling Sid. Wow! You're a comedian as well as a magician.

How did you do it? Easy peasy.

1 Just copy the face drawn below, carefully making sure you have all the lines drawn in the right places.

2 Then fold it in half forwards.

3 Fold it in half again backwards.

4 Fold in half again forwards.

5 Now open the paper and you will find the picture is now the other way up! (Always keep the paper facing away from you and start with the sad face.)

Snap Happy Hypnotist

Now to show your mates that you can be a hypnotist, too. For this you will need three different snap cards and one extra card, the same as one of the other cards. You put this duplicate card in an envelope and seal it. You are now ready to begin.

Ask someone from the audience to come and help you.

Place the three snap cards on a table. Say that you will hypnotise the person into choosing the card you want. Let's say the cards are animal snap cards and you have a camel, a panda and a horse on the table. The duplicate card, sealed in the envelope in full view of everyone, is the panda.

The Trick

Gaze into your helper's eyes and make some wiggly movements with your hands.

Ask the person to pick up two cards. If they pick up the horse and the camel, you put those two aside leaving the panda as the chosen card.

If they pick up the panda and one of the other cards, you tell them to hand you a card. If they give you the panda, then that is the chosen card. If they give you the other card, then they have chosen to keep the panda. In all cases, the panda is the chosen card.

You then get the helper to open the envelope and, wow! it seems you really have hypnotised them!

First Book of Magic 13

 # The Brainy Banana

Does a banana have a brain? Of course it does! You can prove it.

You will need:
1 banana • 6 small pieces of paper • a pencil • an empty glass • a large needle

Show everyone the banana. Then say you are writing numbers 1 to 6 on the six sheets of paper. You fold them, put them in the glass and then ask a helper to pick one out. The helper picks a piece. You unfold it showing the number 3. You then command the banana to split itself into 3 pieces. You ask the helper to peel the banana and there it is, in 3 pieces!

The Secret
You cheat, of course! Beforehand, you have sliced the banana in three pieces with the needle. Get a grown up to help you with this. Just push the needle through the skin into the banana and wiggle it about to make the cut. Then, when you are writing down the numbers, you write 3 on all the pieces of paper!

Knot Magic?

For this, you will need a piece of rope or thick string about 65cms long.

- Tie a simple knot about 7cms from one end. Hold the rope in your left hand with your palm hiding the knot. You are ready to start.

- 1 You tell everyone you are going to make a knot appear by magic.

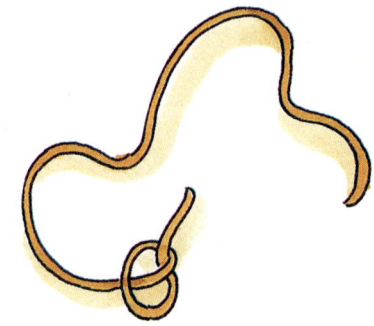

- 2 Transfer the rope into your right hand, making sure the knot is well hidden.

- 3 Lift up the other end of the rope and hold this in your right hand, too.

- 4 Release the unknotted end with a snap. No knot. Hmmm.

- 5 Return the rope to your hand and repeat the move. Still no knot.

- 6 Return the rope once more, say some magic words, then release the secretly knotted end with a snap. Yes, it's there! Magic!

First Book of Magic

Now you see it . . .

These two little tricks will deceive your eyes and everyone else's.

Put a small piece of stiff card on the dotted line in the picture below.

You will need:
card from a cereal packet • a sheet of plain paper • tracing paper

Keep both eyes open and lower your head until the tip of your nose touches the card. See what happens? The dog goes in his basket. What a good boy! Trace and transfer the picture onto plain paper if you want.

16 First Book of Magic

... now you don't

You will need:
tracing paper • a sheet of plain paper • felt tip pens • scissors • glue • sticky tape.

1 Trace the two circles drawn below and transfer them to the plain paper.

2 Colour the clown and the balls but nothing else. Now stick them, back to back, onto some card. Using sticky tape, fix them to the top of your pencil.

3 Rub the pencil between the palms of your hands and see the clown juggle!

First Book of Magic   17

 # Union Jack Mystery

You will need:
3 sheets of A4 plain paper • felt tip pens • a ruler • a pencil • scissors • glue

First, this is the trick:

You hold up a picture of the Union Jack flag which you have drawn on both sides of the A4 sheet of paper.

You ask anyone if they know how many flags make up the Union Jack. The answer is three, the flag of St. George of England, the flag of St. Andrew of Scotland and the flag of St. Patrick of Ireland.

To prove this, you roll the paper flag up into a cone, say some magic words and pull the three flags out of the cone. You then unroll the paper to show it is empty. How did you do it?

18 First Book of Magic

1 Lay 2 A4 sheets of paper (approx. 290 x 210cms) widthways and colour one side of each with the design of the Union Jack.

2 On the back of one of the sheets, draw a 15cm square with your pencil and ruler. This should be 7cm from each side edge and run from the top edge of your paper.

3 Glue the two sheets back to back, but do not glue inside the square. This makes a secret pocket.

4 Now make three little flags of the other countries to fit inside the pocket. Colour them with your felt tip pens.

Practise rolling the flag into a cone and pulling the little flags out. Make sure the secret pocket is always at the top. You will find the point of the cone will help hide the pocket, too.

 # Button Brains

You've had the brainy banana. Here's the brainy button.

Tie a small button onto a piece of string, about 35cms long, and tell your audience that the button has strange powers. Ask it a question that can be answered either 'yes' or 'no'. If it swings in a straight line, the answer is yes. If it swings in a circle, the answer is no.

You cheat again, of course. You can make the button swing in either direction with a very tiny movement of your hand. Practise in front of a mirror until you can move it without anyone knowing.

20 First Book of Magic

Which Way?

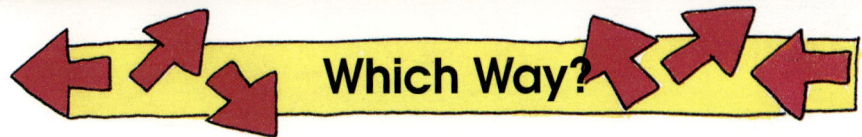

Show your audience a piece of paper with an arrow pointing to the right. Ask them if they can make the arrow point left without touching the paper.

It's easy peasy. Just stand a glass of water in front of the arrow!

Up the Creek

Show your audience a paddle made from the drawings. On it is a rabbit in a canoe without a paddle. You say he is up the creek and can't move as he has no paddle, but you will help him get to the end of the creek with the help of your paddle.

Hold the paddle in your left hand, say a magic word and run a finger of your right hand along the paddle. Wow! The rabbit and the canoe have travelled to the end.

The secret is, you twist the paddle round with your left thumb as you run your finger along it.

Making the Paddle

You will need:
tracing paper • two sheets of plain paper • cardboard from a cereal packet • felt tip pens • glue • scissors

1 Trace the drawings and transfer them to plain paper.

2 Colour the paddles and cut them out.

3 Stick one on a piece of card and cut it out.

4 Stick the other paddle on the back of the card.

5 Practise twisting the paddle until you can do it smoothly.

First Book of Magic   23

Balloon Modelling

Most magicians do a bit of balloon modelling in their act, so why should you be different? Modelling balloons can be bought quite cheaply from toy shops or shops that specialise in balloons. Here's how to make a simple model - a dog.

1 Blow up your balloon. Use a balloon pump if you haven't enough puff. Leave about 6cms (2") at the end. This gives the air somewhere to go when you start to model. If you blow your balloon right up, it will burst when you start twisting it. Aaah.

3 Starting at the knotted end, make a twist about 6cms along the balloon.

2 Knot the end so the air cannot escape.

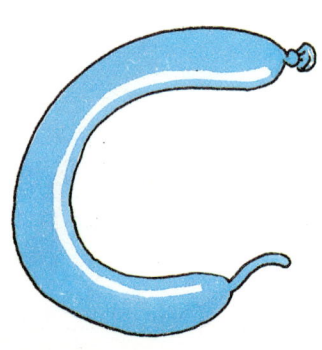

4 Make another twist the same length.

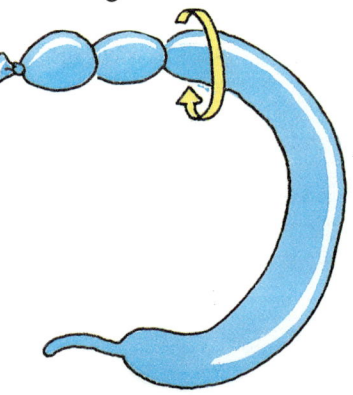

5 Holding tightly onto these twists, turn them on their side and make a third twist.

6 Twist at the second and third ones round the first one and you have the dog's head.

7 Moving down the balloon about 8cms, you make two further twists for the front legs.

8 Then make two further twists for the back legs. You put these where you like, depending how long you want your dog to be.

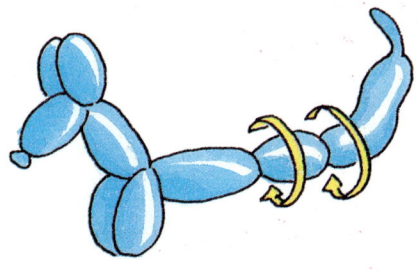

9 Hey Presto. There's your dog!

First Book of Magic   25

 # Royal Workout - The Kings

This is an optical illusion for you to try out on your mates.

You will need:
tracing paper • stiff paper or thin card • scissors • a pencil • felt tip pens

Trace and transfer both pictures onto plain paper. Colour them in. Then cut them out.

First Book of Magic

Royal Workout - The Story

1 Hold the King of Diamonds in your left hand and the King of Hearts in your right. Ask the audience who is bigger. They will say the King of Hearts.

2 Say the King of Diamonds didn't like this answer so he decided to make himself bigger. He started doing all sorts of exercises, running, weight lifting and such to make himself bigger. And when he had finished he found he had. Swop the Kings over and the King of Diamonds will look bigger.

3 You then say the King of Hearts didn't like this, so he started doing lots of exercises to make himself bigger, too, and when he finished he was. Swop them again. But really all this exercise was a waste of time for the Kings were really the same size all the time. Put them together and prove it!

First Book of Magic   27

Fun with Shadows

Making shadow shapes is closely related to magic, so here are a few to try. You will need a plain wall or sheet of paper for the shadow, light from a torch and, oh, a dark room! See if you can make up a story about the shapes, too.

1 The elephant. Make his trunk swing.

3 The bird. It flies, too, if you wiggle your fingers.

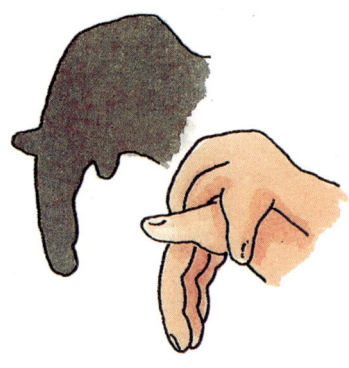

2 The dog. Open your bottom fingers and he'll bark.

4 How about a rabbit? All magicians have a rabbit.

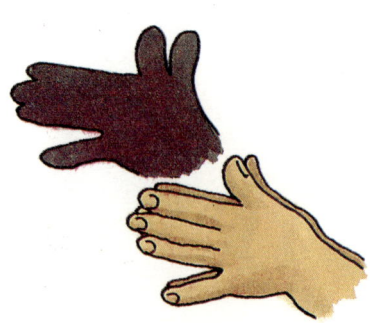

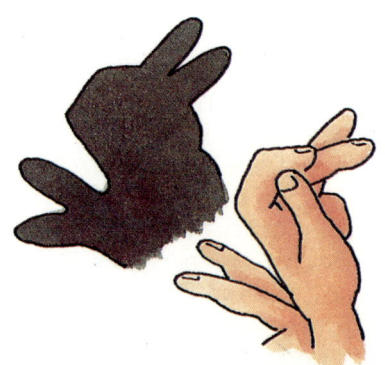

5 Here's a seagull.

7 A beautiful swan

6 And a slithery snake, oo..er. Wiggle your arm to make it look real.

8 And what is this? A goat or maybe a long-necked giraffe.

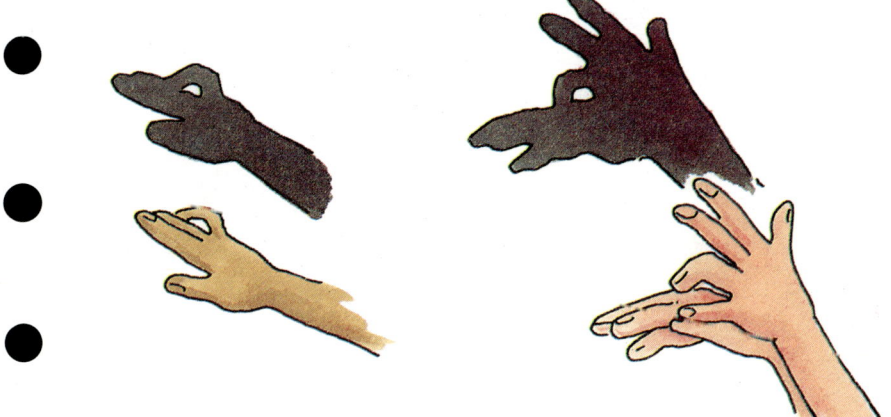

Saw the Dog in Half

You will need:
an envelope • a piece of plain card or stiff paper • felt tip pens • a pencil • coloured sticky paper • scissors

1 Copy the picture of the sleeping dog onto your piece of stiff paper or card. Colour the picture and cut it out.

2 Stick the envelope down and trim it, so it is just a bit shorter than your dog.

3 Cut two slits in the back of the envelope, large enough for the dog to slide through.

4 Decorate the front of the envelope with shapes made from the sticky paper.

30 First Book of Magic

1 Tell your audience that they may have heard of the illusion of sawing the lady in half, but you are going to saw a dog in half instead.

2 Show everyone your cabinet and your dog.

3 Slide the dog inside the cabinet, making sure it comes out of one slit and back in the other.

4 Cut the cabinet, sliding the scissors behind the dog, so it remains unharmed.
The cabinet falls in half and you reveal the dog, whole and, would you believe, still asleep!

Oath of Secrecy

You may have heard all of this before, but it is important that you keep secret how you do all your magic tricks. If you do, you can keep everyone guessing. Because, even if people think they know what's being done, they don't actually know for sure. But if you've told them, they will know and probably just make fun of you! So don't give in! Keep it secret. It's more fun for everyone then!

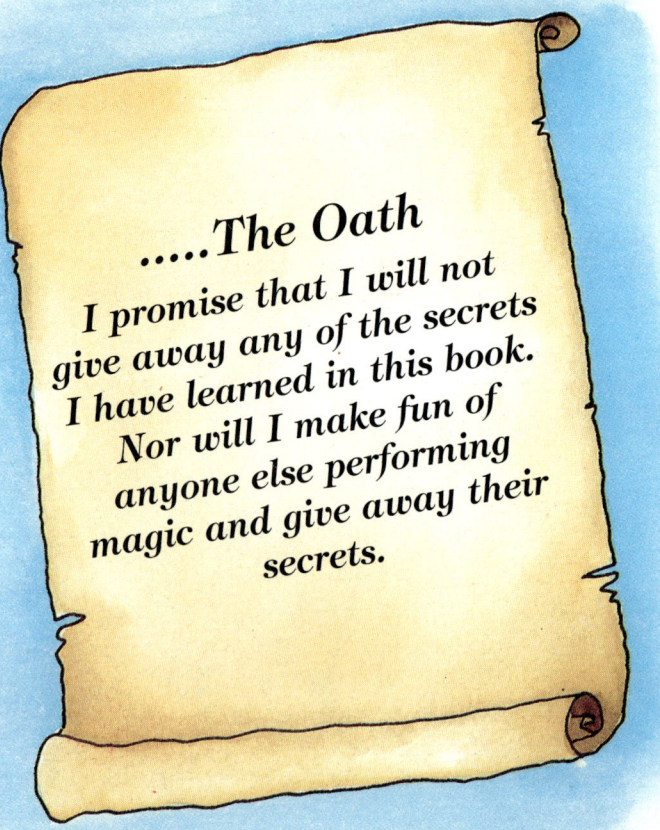

.....The Oath

I promise that I will not give away any of the secrets I have learned in this book. Nor will I make fun of anyone else performing magic and give away their secrets.